LET'S INVESTIGATE
Numbers

LET'S INVESTIGATE
Numbers

By Marion Smoothey

Illustrated by Ted Evans

MARSHALL CAVENDISH
NEW YORK · LONDON · TORONTO · SYDNEY

Library Edition Published 1993

© Marshall Cavendish Corporation 1993

Published by Marshall Cavendish Corporation
2415 Jerusalem Avenue
PO Box 587
North Bellmore
New York 11710

Series created by Graham Beehag Book Design

Library of Congress Cataloging-in-Publication Data

Smoothey, Marion, 1943-
    Numbers / by Marion Smoothey; illustrated by Ted Evans.
        p. cm.. -- (Let's Investigate)
    Includes index.
    Summary: Introduces simple math concepts through a variety of
problems, games, and activities.
    ISBN 1-85435-457-4   ISBN 1-85435-455-8 (set)
    1. Counting -- Juvenile literature. 2. Number concept -- Juvenile
literature. [1. Number concept. 2. Mathematics. 3. Mathematical
recreations.] I. Evans, Ted ill. II. Title. III. Series:
    Smoothey, Marion, 1943- Let's Investigate.
    QA113.S625 1992   92-5172
    513--dc20   CIP
                                                      AC

Printed in Malaysia
Bound in the United States

Contents

Learning to Count

*"One, two, three, four, five
Once I caught a fish alive"*

Ordinary counting numbers, or integers, are among the first words we learn to say as children. You can probably count to ten in a foreign language even if you cannot speak it properly. So it will probably surprise you that it took early people many thousands of years to discover the idea of counting. It was not until they began to settle in villages and to farm and trade that numbers became important to them.

Our word "calculate" comes from the Latin word for pebble, "calculus."

In the early days of counting people used their fingers, or carved notches on a stick, or moved a pile of pebbles. Since then we have learned to use the power of numbers to understand and explore first the seas and now the galaxies.

We use numbers for money when we buy things at home and abroad. Cartographers use numbers to make the maps which enable us to find our way when we travel. Engineers use numbers to design and build buildings and machines. Scientists use numbers as tools to try to understand the forces of nature that govern our world.

8

Some of the early mathematicians thought that numbers had magic powers. Some people still believe that seven is a lucky number. It is certainly true that once we can grasp the idea of using numbers we can do a great many things which we could not do before.

Writing Figures

● What do you think this chart shows?

Arabic	1	2	3	4	5	6	7	8	9	10	20	50	100
Egyptian	I	II	III	IIII	III / II	III / III	IIII / III	IIII / IIII	III / III / III	∩	∩∩	∩∩∩ / ∩∩	@
Babylonian	Y	YY	YYY	YYYY	YYY / YY	YYY / YYY	YYYY / YYY	YYYY / YYY	YYYY / YYY	<	<<	<<< / <<	∇
Roman	I	II	III	IIII	V	VI	VII	VIII	IX	X	XX	L	C
Greek	A	B	Γ	Δ	E	F	Z	H	θ	I	K	N	P
Mayan	•	••	•••	••••	—	≐	⸛	⸬	⸬•	=	⊙	⊞	⊖

When writing down numbers, we use a sign, or symbol, for each number instead of writing the word.

Symbol	1	2	3	4	5	6	7	8	9
Word	one	two	three	four	five	six	seven	eight	nine

Our number symbols are called Arabic, because the Arabs began to use them many years ago. However, the idea for the signs originated in India. The early Hindu signs were gradually altered over the years, first by the Arabs and later by Europeans, until they became the ones we know today.

It was not until the early fifteenth century that Arabic numerals were widely used in Europe. The knowledge of them was brought back from eastern lands by traders, travelers and soldiers.

Before that time, the numerals of the ancient Romans were still used.

● You can still find Roman numerals today sometimes. Where?

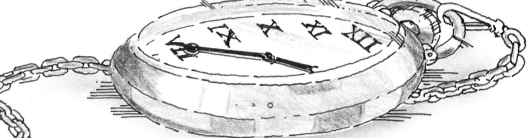

10

The ancient civilizations of the Mayas of Central America, the Egyptians, and the Babylonians of the Middle East each had their own systems for recording numbers.

Study the table on page 9 which shows the different systems.

● How is the Arabic system different from all the others? Is this an advantage or a disadvantage?

● What are these numbers in Arabic?

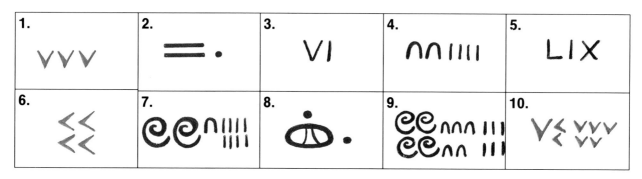

1.	2.	3.	4.	5.
VVV	=.	VI	∩∩IIIII	LIX
6.	7.	8.	9.	10.
<< <<	℮℮∩IIIII	⊕.	℮℮∩∩∩III ℮℮∩∩ III	V< VVV VV

Puzzle

● What ten digit number will fit into the squares so that: the digit in the 0 square is the same as the total number of 0's in the whole number and the digit in the 1 square shows the total number of 1's in the whole number?

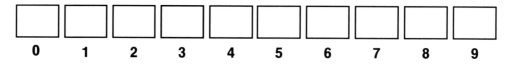

Discovering Zero

Perhaps when you thought about the differences between the Arabic system and the others, you noticed that the Arabic is the only one which uses a zero to form ten and one hundred. A zero used in this way becomes a very useful symbol. It saves us from needing new symbols for 10, 100, 1,000 and so on.

To record 10, we simply move the 1 to the left – from the units place to the tens place

tens	units
1	1×10

and mark the fact that there are no units with a zero.

tens	units
1	0

To record 100, we move the 1 two places to the left and mark the empty tens and units places with a zero for each.

hundreds	tens	units
1	10×10 0	1×10 0

We can do this as many times as we like, so that we can write very large numbers in a short way. Also, using the zero as a marker helps us to add and subtract.

● Which is easier?

15 + 206	XV + CCVI	N CC

Did you know?

The earliest written numbers which have been discovered so far were used in ancient Egypt and in Mesopotamia five thousand years ago.

The Importance of Place

12

In our number system, the position of the numbers is important. 51 is different from 15. 51 is also different from 501. The zero acts as a marker; it tells us there are no tens; there are five hundreds and one unit.

By using zero and the position of numbers, we can represent any number, however huge, with just ten different symbols. Although the Arabic symbols are harder to learn at first, because they do not look like the numbers they represent, the use of zero and place value means you only have to learn ten signs.

15 ⇐ **1 ten and 5 units**

51 ⇐ **5 tens and 1 unit**

501 ⇐ **5 hundreds, 0 tens and 1 unit**

Arabic 1,873 = Roman MDCCCLXXIII

Arabic 785,003,200 = Egyptian

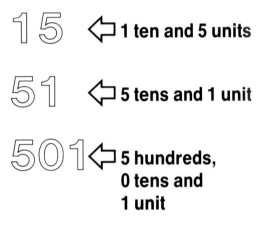

The Egyptians had different symbols for 10, 100, 1000 and so on up to 1 million.

1	10	10^2	10^3	10^4	10^5	10^6
I	∩	℮	𝍏	⌐	ഖ	𝀝

The Babylonians made marks in clay tablets with a special wedge shaped stick. When the wedge pointed down it meant 1; when it pointed to the left it meant 10.

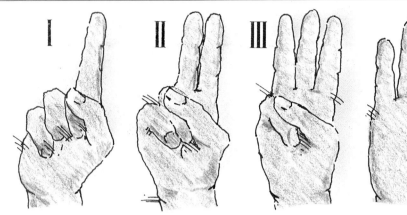

Roman numerals look like the fingers of the hands held up for counting. The symbol IV (four) came into use later times.

● Can you design some symbols and invent a new number system? How many symbols will you need? Can you make them easy to remember? Will you need an empty place marker symbol?

● Try using your system to write 15097 and to add 67 to 139. How about subtracting 29 from 735. Difficult isn't it?

The Mayas sometimes used the idea of multiplication to write large numbers. It is time consuming to write a long row of symbols. Also it is difficult to count. To write 100 they used the symbol for 5 and the symbol for 20. When placed one above the other it meant 5 multiplied by 20.

Below: This is an example of an invented number system based on a stroke for 1, and a circle for 5.

1	2	3	4	5
I	+	✳	✴	O
6	7	8	9	10
OI	O+	O✳	O✴	OO
11				20
II				OO OO
OOI				OO OO

Puzzle

A space traveler found a capsule with these symbols on it.

● What were the next two?
☆ **Hint: You need to *reflect* on it!**

Using an Abacus

As people began to trade and calculate more frequently, they looked for ways of making counting easier. An early counting aid, and one which is still used today, particularly in Far Eastern countries, is the abacus.

The simplest form of abacus is a board with grooves to represent the columns for units, tens, hundreds, etc. Up to 9 pebbles may be placed in each column to represent a number.

To add 374 and 25,
place pebbles to represent 374

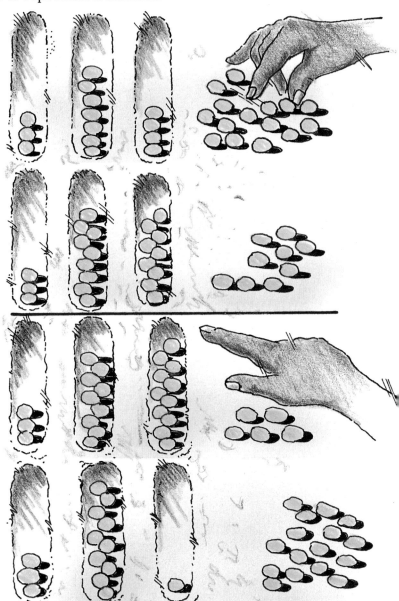

Now add another 25. Place
2 pebbles in the middle column
to represent two tens. Place
5 pebbles in the right hand
column to represent five units.
Read the answer.

To add 374 and 27 is
a little more complicated.
Begin as before.

No column may have more than
9 pebbles, so replace the 11 unit
pebbles with 1 ten pebble and
1 unit pebble.

14

This gives 10 pebbles in the ten column, which is not allowed. Change the 10 tens into 1 hundred. Now read the answer.

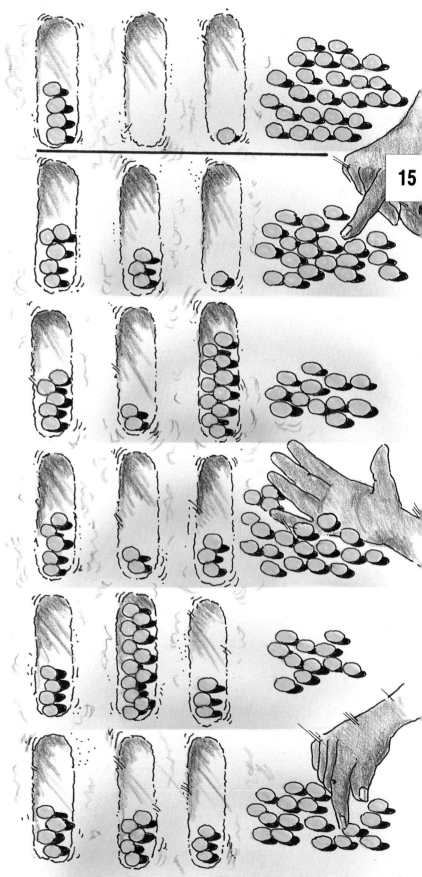

Subtraction is similar. Follow the diagrams to figure out 531 − 78 on an abacus.

Start with the units column. You cannot take 8 unit stones away. Change 1 ten stone into 10 unit stones.

Take away 8 unit stones.

Now do the tens column. There are not 7 ten stones to take away so change 1 hundred stone into 10 ten stones.

Take away 7 ten stones. Read the answer.

Use graph paper and counters to make yourself a counting board and try these problems. Or you can travel back in time by using pebbles and grooves in sand or earth.

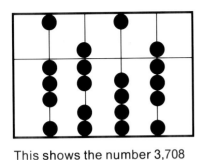

This shows the number 3,708

Modern Chinese and Japanese abacuses are beads on wires set in a metal frame. The frame has a horizontal divider. The four beads in each column below the divider are worth one each; the one bead in each column above the divider is worth five. To represent a number, move the required number of beads toward the divider.

To add 14 to 3,708 on this kind of abacus, first add on the 4 units.

$4+8=12=1$ **ten** and 2 **units**, so push one 1 bead in the tens column toward the divider. In the units column, move 1 one bead and the five bead away from the divider to display 2 units.

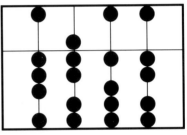

Now change the tens column. Move one 1 bead in the tens column toward the divider and read the answer.

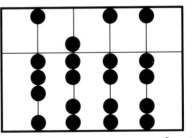

To add 97 to 3,708 requires more mental arithmetic! Begin with the **units** column.

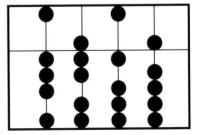

$8+7=15=1$ **ten** and 5 **units**

Next deal with the **tens.**

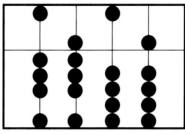

In the tens column 1 + 9 = 10 = 1 hundred and 0 tens

Read off the answer, **3,805** from the abacus.

If you are not used to using an abacus, it probably seems difficult and slow. In fact, when used by a skilled operator, it is a very efficient calculating aid.

Sometimes counting frames with bright colored beads are given to small children as toys. You can practice doing some addition sums with one of these. See if you can get so quick that you can beat someone with an electronic calculator.

● With a washed frozen food tray, a piece of cardboard, some string and a few plastic straws you can make an abacus.

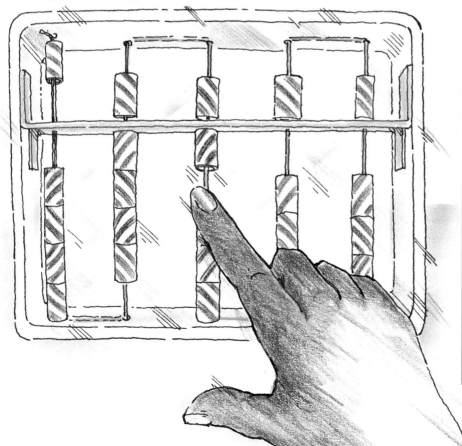

Use your abacus to subtract (take away) 23 from 146.

Subtract 3 **units**

Subtract 2 **tens**

Now try 146 − 53

Number Bases

- Look at the illustration above. When does $10 + 3 = 1$?

Look again at the table of different number systems on page 9.

- At what number do the Roman and Mayan systems first change the kind of symbol they use?

- What happens at the number 10 in each of the Egyptian, Babylonian and Roman systems?

- Why should the numbers 5 and 10 be special to these people?

- Which culture made 20 a special number?

- What parts of their body do you think they used for counting?

The number which is used to form a group in a number system is called the base. Today we usually work in base ten, sometimes called the denary system. We count up to nine and then when we get to one more we group the $9 + 1$ as 10.

We then carry on with 11, (1 ten and 1 unit), 12, (1 ten and 2 units), and so on until we have two groups of ten which we write as 20) (2 tens and 0 units).

The Babylonians used 60 as their base. Although this seems a large, awkward number to work with, we still use it when dividing hours into minutes, and minutes into seconds. It was also the Babylonians who divided a circle into 360 degrees.

- How many 60's in 360?

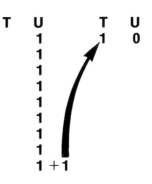

T	U		T	U
1			1	0
1				
1				
1				
1				
1				
1				
1				
1	+1			

Long, long ago, in the realms of the imagination, lived the Quaterns. The four holy priests of the tribe were each the guardian of one of the four sacred groves of four holy trees. Each tree bore four fruits which it was forbidden, on the threat of death, to pick. When the fruits ripened and fell to the earth, each one split to reveal four seeds.

Among the Quaterns, only the priests knew the secret of counting. They used the seed as 1 and grouped them into f's, t's, g's and p's. 4 seeds = 1 fruit, 4 fruits = 1 tree and so on. How many seeds = 1 priest?

● Can you work out the answers to these Quatern sums in base ten?

1.

P	G	T	F	S
		1	0	3 +
			2	1
1	**3**	**0**		

2.

P	G	T	F	S
2	0	2	1	1 +
	3	1	3	2
3	0	0	0	3

3.

P	G	T	F	S
2	0	2	1	1 −
	1	0	1	
2	0	1	1	0

4.

T	F	S
	3	1 ×
		3
2	1	3

● Try making up a story of your own to explain the use of a different base and use it to do some simple sums.

Computer Numbers

Computers use the number 2 as their base. They work on the binary system. In base two each column is worth twice as much as the column to its right.

Instead of	10000's	1000's	100's	10's	and 1's
the column headings are	16's	8's	4's	2's	and 1's

Base two would not be an easy base for us to use because it takes a long time to write numbers in binary.

21 in base ten is 10101 in base two

1733 in base ten is 11011000101 in base two

Because computers have such large memories and work very fast, the length of the numbers is only a small disadvantage to them. A much more important *advantage* is that a binary system only needs two symbols. The 1 and the 0 can be represented by an electric pulse being ON or OFF.

You could represent a binary number by a series of lamps being switched on or off.

● You can make a simple binary calculator for yourself to see the way a computer counts.

All you need are a thin stick, like a knitting needle or a drinking straw, some paper and a hole punch.

1. Cut seven pieces of paper, about 1″ square.

2. Punch two holes in the top of each so that you can thread them on to the stick.

3. Write a 1 on the top side of each square and a 0 on the underneath of each.

4. In the bottom corner of each square, in small figures write the binary column headings 1, 2, 4, 8, 16, 32 and 64.

To do the sum 13 + 17, first write down 13 and 17 as binary numbers. 13 = 1101 (1 one, 0 twos, 1 four and 1 eight) and 17 = 10001 (1 one, 0 twos, 0 fours, 0 eights and 1 sixteen) Set the counter to 1101.

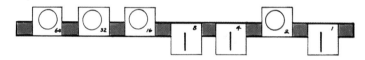

Now start adding 10001 from the right hand side. One 1 added to the 1 already showing changes the 1 to zero and the 2 to one.

The next three zeros make no change to the calculator.

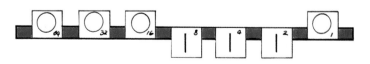

The final one on the left hand side changes the 16 square on the calculator from zero to one.

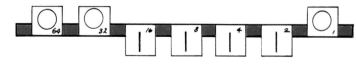

Now read off the number 11110. In base 10 that is, from the *right hand side*, 0 + 2 + 4 + 8 + 16 = 30

Now try $27 + 42$.

1. First work out 27 and 42 in binary.

27 is 16 8 4 2 1
      1 1 0 1 1
$(16+8+0+2+1)$

42 is 32 16 8 4 2 1
      1 0 1 0 1 0
$(32+0+8+0+2+0)$

2. Set the counter to 11011.

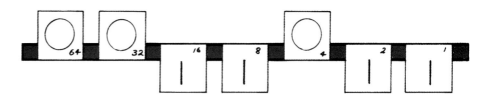

3. Starting from the right hand side.
10101**0** zero makes no change to the ones.
1010**1**0 one changes the twos to 0 and the fours to 1.

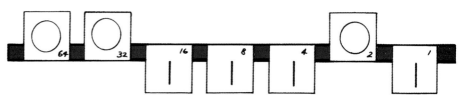

101**0**10 zero makes no change to the fours.
10**1**010 one changes the eights to 0, the sixteens to 0 and the thirty-twos to 1.

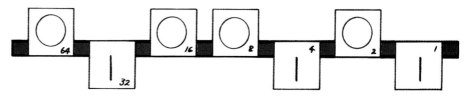

1**0**1010 zero makes no change to the sixteens.
101010 one changes the thirty-twos to 0 and the sixty-fours to 1.

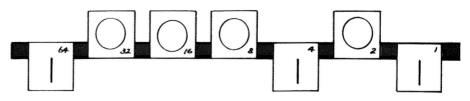

4. Now read off the answer – 1000101
which in base 10 is $64+0+0+0+4+0+1=69$

● Try some simple sums of your own. What is the biggest number in base 10 that you can display in base 2 with your seven pieces of paper?

Odd and Even Numbers

23

- What would be the number of the third house on this side of the road in this street?

- Which house would house number 15 be opposite to?

- How can you tell if these groups of dots are odd or even numbers?

One way is to mark them off in pairs to see if an odd one is left over.

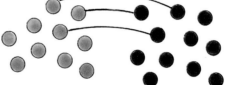

If the pairs are arranged neatly, it is easy to see whether a large number is odd or even.

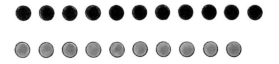

Try throwing two dice and adding the scores. Record your results in a table, using one color for odd numbers and another for even numbers. Make about twenty throws.

Red die	Blue die	TOTAL	Odd or Even
4	3	7	ODD
3	2	5	ODD
1	1	2	EVEN
6	1	7	ODD
2	4	6	EVEN

24

● What rules can you make about the results of adding two even numbers, two odd numbers, an odd and an even number? Record your results in a table like this.

+	ODD	EVEN
ODD		
EVEN		

Cut some odd and even numbers out of graph paper. Try joining them together in pairs (adding them).

● Can you explain why the rules in your table must always work?

A game for two players

Draw a board of nine squares. Mark the points A and B. Place a counter on A. Each player takes turns to move along one side of a square. The player who makes the final move of the counter to B is the winner.

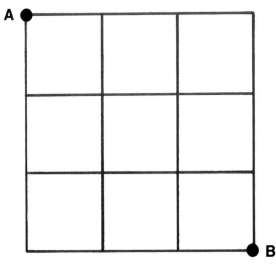

- **1.** Can you predict which player will win?

- **2.** If you add a rule that no move may take the counter further away from B, who will always win?

- **3.** Change the rules so that each player moves along two sides of a square at each turn. Who wins now?

- Investigate who wins when you change the starting position.

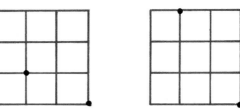

- **4.** What has this got to do with odd and even?

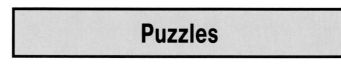

Puzzles

- **5.** What four different odd numbers added together make 20?

- **6.** Which two different odd numbers and two different even numbers make 10?

- **7.** What do you need to add to any odd number to make it even?

- **8.** What is the smallest number you can multiply by to make any odd number into an even one?

- **9.** If two numbers multiplied together produce an odd number, what do you know about them both?

- **10.** If you halve an even number can you say whether the result will be odd or even?

- **11.** What four consecutive odd numbers make 80 when added together?

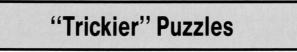

"Trickier" Puzzles

- **12.** What number becomes even when you take away 1?

- What odd number becomes even when you take away 2?

Prime Numbers

2, 3, 5, 7, 11, 13, 17, 19...

26

What will be the next number in this list?

You might be tempted to answer 21, because at first glance it looks like a list of the odd numbers. If you look more closely you will notice that it begins with 2, an even number, and that 9 and 15 are missing.

In fact the answer is 23.

Can you see why?

Consider the numbers which have been left out.

4, 6, 8, 9, 10, 12, 14, 15, 16, 18

All, except 9 and 15, are even; they can all be divided exactly by 2. 2 is a **factor** of 4, 6, 8, 10, 12, 14, 16, 18.

That leaves 9 and 15. 2 is not a factor but 3 is.
$9 = 3 \times 3$ and $15 = 3 \times 5$

Returning to the original list 2, 3, 5, 7, 11, 13, 17, 19..., you can see that none of these numbers have any factors except themselves and 1

$2 = 2 \times 1$
$3 = 3 \times 1$
$5 = 5 \times 1$ and so on.

Numbers which have no other factors except themselves and 1 are called primes.

A prime number cannot be divided exactly by any other number except 1.

1 is not counted as a prime.

Investigation

Write down the prime numbers which are less than 10, less than 20, less than 30 and less than 40.

● How many are there below 10, below 20, below 30 and below 40?

● Can you predict how many primes there are up to number 100?

You could set out your work like this.

Primes up to 10

2, 3, 5, 7,   TOTAL 4

Primes up to 20

as above plus 11, 13, 17, 19   TOTAL ?

Primes up to 30

and so on.

You will have seen that the number of primes, and the frequency at which they occur, does not fall into in any pattern.

Even with the most sophisticated computer, we will never be able to predict the total number of primes which will occur between any two numbers. We can only find out by identifying them and counting them.

Although a computer can do this much quicker than we can, it still has to use some way of deciding which numbers are prime and then counting them up to see how many there are. Programs to do this are based on a method which was first thought of over 2000 years ago by the Greek mathematician, Eratosthenes.

The Sieve of Eratosthenes

To find all the primes from 1 to 100 draw a 10 by 10 square and fill in the numbers 2 to 100 as shown below.

You sieve out the primes by shading all the numbers which are not primes.

First shade all the numbers, except 2 itself, which are **multiples** of 2. That is all the numbers which 2 divides exactly, with no remainder. This shades all the even numbers.

	2	3	4	5	6	7	8	9	10
11	12	13	14	15	16	17	18	19	20
21	22	23	24	25	26	27	28	29	30
31	32	33	34	35	36	37	38	39	40
41	42	43	44	45	46	47	48	49	50
51	52	53	54	55	56	57	58	59	60
61	62	63	64	65	66	67	68	69	70
71	72	73	74	75	76	77	78	79	80
81	82	83	84	85	86	87	88	89	90
91	92	93	94	95	96	97	98	99	100

Next shade all the multiples of 3, except 3 itself.

The multiples of 4 are already shaded. They are all even because 4 itself is a multiple of 2.

The multiples of 5 are shaded next. Continue working through the multiples of the numbers up to 10. You do not need to go beyond 10. 10 × 10 = 100, so all the possible multiples will have been shaded by then.

If you are uncertain of your multiplication tables, you can complete the sieve by counting in a pattern. For example, for multiples of 6 you count on 6 squares at a time from 6 and shade each sixth square. As the patterns build up, it is easy to see where the shading goes.

You should now be able to list and total the primes from 2 to 100.

● Is there any pattern in the number of squares between the primes?

Answers on page 30

Testing whether or not a number is prime

Is 263 a prime number?

To find out we need to test for prime **factors**.

When a number is divided by a factor, there is no remainder. A prime factor is a factor which is a prime number.

    2 and 3 are both prime factors of 6.
    $6 \div 2 = 3$ and $6 \div 3 = 2$

Testing for prime factors of 263
2 is not a factor, because 263 ends in an odd number,

3 is not a factor, because $2 + 6 + 3 = 11$ which is not divisible by 3. (The sum of the digits of any number which is divisible by 3 is itself divisible by 3; for example, 216)

5 is not a factor, because 263 does not end in 0 or 5. (See the pattern of 5's in your sieve.)

1. Try 7.

```
      37 r 4
7 │ 263
    21
    ──
    53
    49
    ──
     4
```

7 is not a factor.

3. How about 13?

```
       20 r 3
13│ 263
    26
    ──
    03
    00
    ──
     3
```

2. The next possible prime factor is 11.

```
      23 r 10
11│ 263
    22
    ──
    43
    33
    ──
    10
```

11 is not a factor.

4. Try 17

```
      15 r 8
17│ 263
    17
    ──
    93
    85
    ──
     8
```

We do not need to test for any more factors. $17 \times 17 = 289$, which is more than 263, so we have covered all the possibilities.

263 is a prime number.

Were you right?

	2	3	4	5	6	7	8	9	10
11	12	13	14	15	16	17	18	19	20
21	22	23	24	25	26	27	28	29	30
31	32	33	34	35	36	37	38	39	40
41	42	43	44	45	46	47	48	49	50
51	52	53	54	55	56	57	58	59	60
61	62	63	64	65	66	67	68	69	70
71	72	73	74	75	76	77	78	79	80
81	82	83	84	85	86	87	88	89	90
91	92	93	94	95	96	97	98	99	100

There are 25 primes between 2 and 100. There is no pattern in the squares between them.

More testing for primes

Which of these numbers are primes ?

68,   253,   1705,   73,   27,   1309,   283,   119,   221

We can take out some right away. We can see they have factors.

68 is even, so it has 2 as a factor.

27 the sum of the digits is 9. This is divisible by 3, so 3 is a factor.

1705 ends in 5, so it has 5 as a factor.

Now we must test the rest using the prime factors of 7 and above.

$$
253 \qquad 7 \overline{\smash{\big)}\,253} \;\; \overset{36\ r1}{}
$$

```
         36 r1                      23
     7 | 253                   11 | 253
       21                          22
       43                          33
       42                          33
        1                           0
```

11 is a factor so 253 is not prime. (You may have already known this, because the sum of the outside digits is equal to the inside one.)

73

We stop here because $11 \times 11 = 121$ so we must have tested all the possible factors for 73. 73 is prime.

● Now you test the remaining four numbers: 1309, 119, 283 and 221.

Did you know?

A computer at the University of California took two months in 1979 to find what was then the biggest known prime number. It had 13,395 digits.

On August 6, 1989 in Santa Clara, California, the Amdahl 1200 supercomputer produced a prime number of 65,087 digits.

There can never be a largest prime number. There will always be another one which is bigger.

Think about it this way.

Imagine the largest prime number P. Multiply together all the prime factors up to P and add 1 to the answer.

$(2 \times 3 \times 5 \times 7 \times 11....... \times P) + 1$

The new number is either a prime or not. If it is a prime, then P is not the largest prime. If the new number is not a prime, then it must have a prime factor which is not P or any of the prime factors before it, because all these factors leave a remainder of 1. So there must be another prime factor larger than P and P is not the largest prime.

Puzzles

● Choose any number, multiply it by 6, then either add 1 to the result or subtract 1. Does this always produce a prime number?

● Can you find four prime numbers which when multiplied together with any 2-digit number xy will turn it into the 6-digit number xyxyxy?

FRACTIONS

At the beginning of this book, you read that it was not until people began to settle and farm and trade that numbers became important. Problems soon began to arise which could not be solved with just the counting numbers.

Suppose a man had a flock of 50 sheep, which he wished to be shared equally among his children. If he had two children, there would be no problem. Each child would have 25 sheep. But what if he had three children, or four?

This problem could only be solved by compromise, or by some dead sheep! But when it came to such things as fields or sacks of grain, it made sense to divide them into equal parts. People began to use the idea of fractions.

We use fractions all the time in everyday life.

Sometimes we are not very careful in what we say. Fractions mean equal parts. Two halves must be exactly equal. If they are not equal they are not halves.

"Your half is bigger than mine!"

● Which of these diagrams are actually divided into the fractions with which they are labeled?

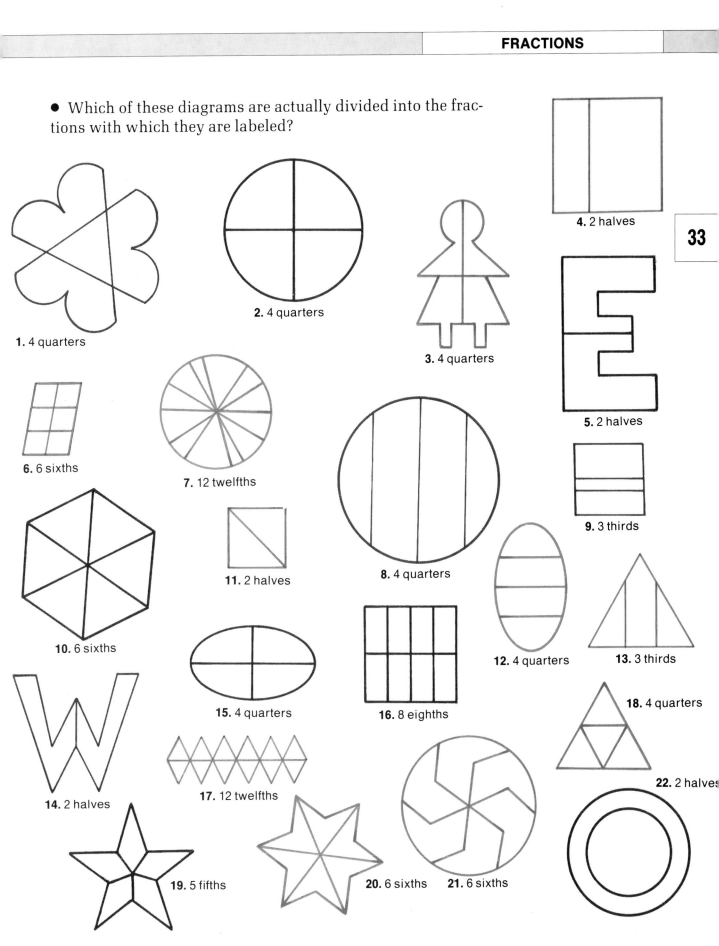

1. 4 quarters

2. 4 quarters

3. 4 quarters

4. 2 halves

5. 2 halves

6. 6 sixths

7. 12 twelfths

8. 4 quarters

9. 3 thirds

10. 6 sixths

11. 2 halves

12. 4 quarters

13. 3 thirds

14. 2 halves

15. 4 quarters

16. 8 eighths

17. 12 twelfths

18. 4 quarters

19. 5 fifths

20. 6 sixths

21. 6 sixths

22. 2 halves

Trace and divide these shapes into the required fractions. For some of them, it is easier to cut them out and fold them. **Answers on page 37**

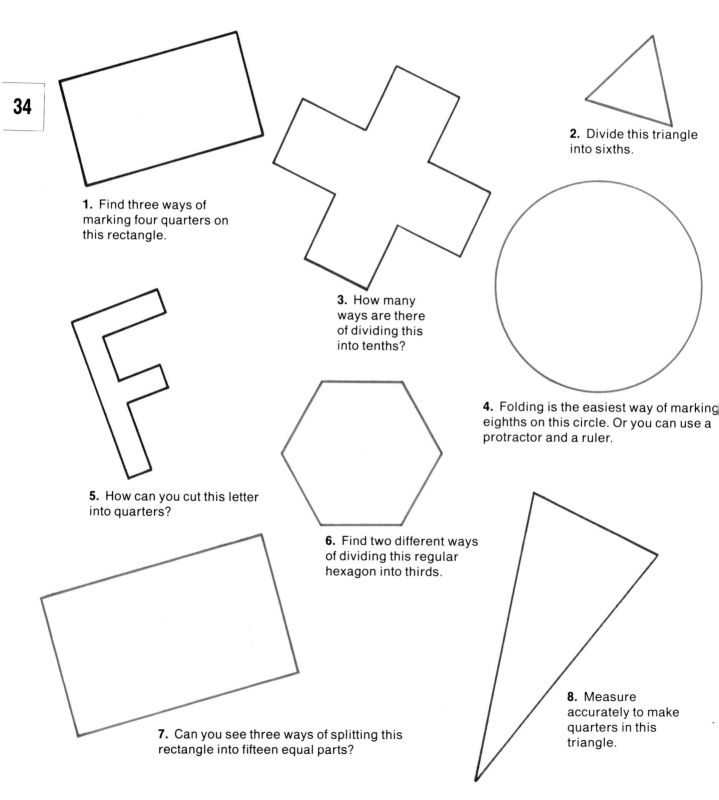

1. Find three ways of marking four quarters on this rectangle.

2. Divide this triangle into sixths.

3. How many ways are there of dividing this into tenths?

4. Folding is the easiest way of marking eighths on this circle. Or you can use a protractor and a ruler.

5. How can you cut this letter into quarters?

6. Find two different ways of dividing this regular hexagon into thirds.

7. Can you see three ways of splitting this rectangle into fifteen equal parts?

8. Measure accurately to make quarters in this triangle.

Investigation

Answer on page 36

How many ways can you halve a square?

You need lots of scrap paper; newspaper will do. Cut out ten squares with sides about 5″ long. Using folding, a ruler, compasses or any other means, cut or shade each square into two exactly equal halves.

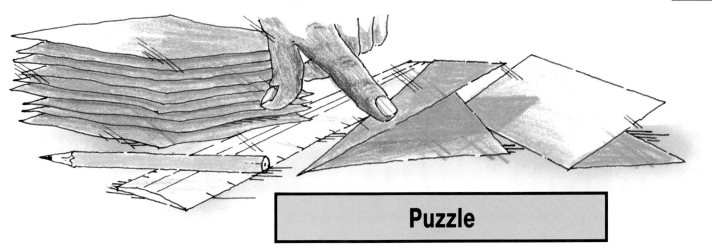

Puzzle

Answer on page 38

Below are four diagrams of a hexagon. One is whole; the others are divided into halves, thirds and sixths. Trace them and cut them into pieces. Use all the pieces to make one large hexagon.

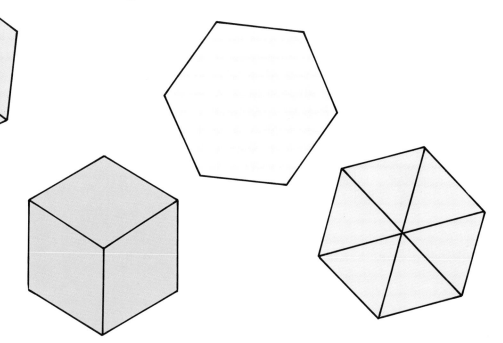

Halving a square

There are an infinite number of ways of doing this. Did you use any of these?

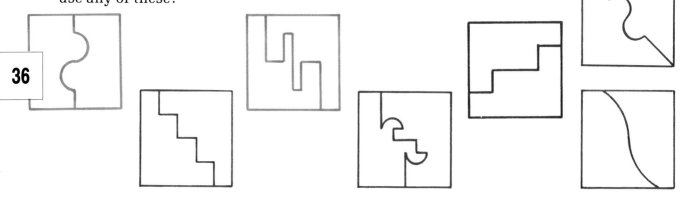

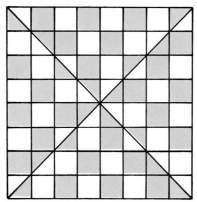

A good way of checking cut out halves is to lay one on top of another. They should fit exactly.

If you divide the square into smaller squares or triangles, you can make many intricate patterns by shading half of them.

Now try halving a rectangular piece of paper. A piece of your tablet paper is a good size to work with.

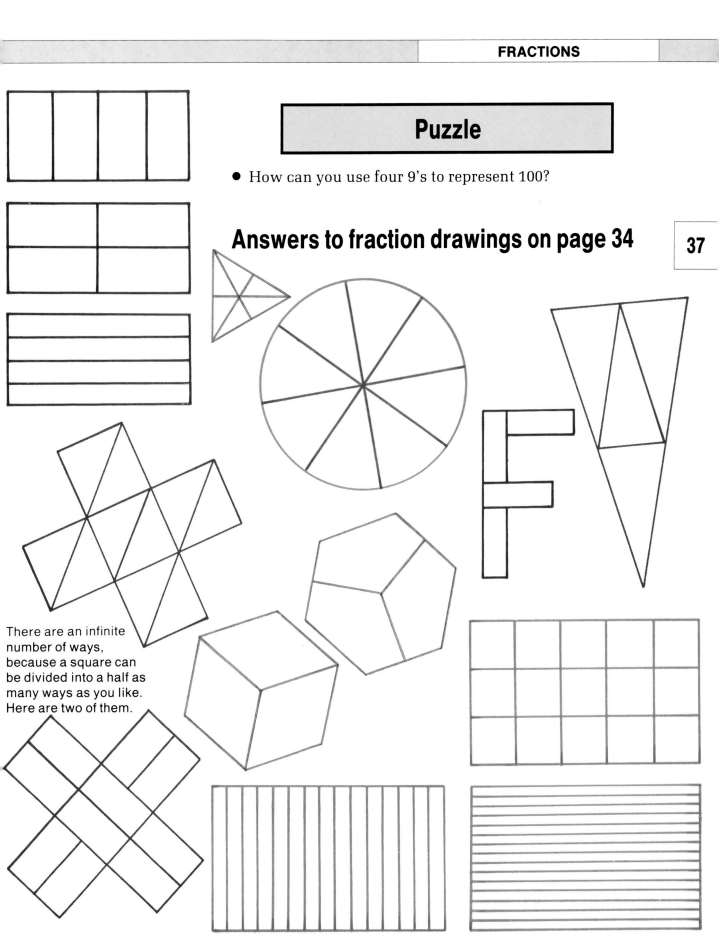

Puzzle

● How can you use four 9's to represent 100?

Answers to fraction drawings on page 34

There are an infinite number of ways, because a square can be divided into a half as many ways as you like. Here are two of them.

Answer

Here is one possible solution to the puzzle on page 35. There are many more ways of arranging the pieces to fit.

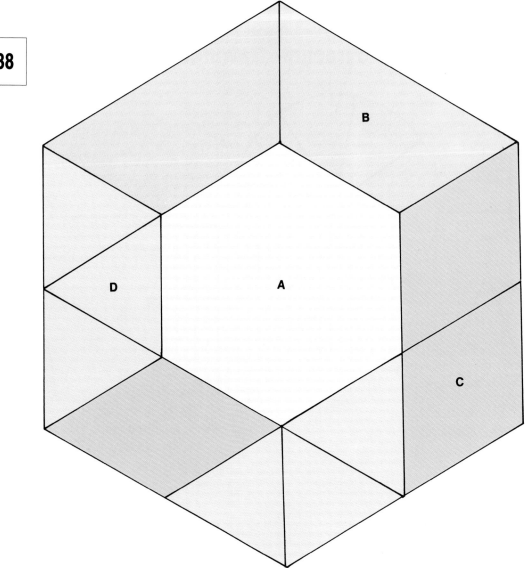

● What fraction of the NEW hexagon are pieces A, B, C and D?

☆ **Hint – remember that there were four equal hexagons to start with.**

Equivalent fractions

Look carefully at this rectangle. How many equal pieces is it divided into?

1.

You can answer eight equal pieces, or eight $\frac{1}{8}$'s

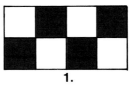

2.

If you rearrange the colored squares you can see four equal pieces or four $\frac{1}{4}$'s

3.   **4.**

or two equal pieces or two $\frac{1}{2}$'s.

Each answer is correct. When we are dealing with fractions, there is often more than one way of describing the parts of a particular whole.

If you look at the diagrams you can see that
$\frac{2}{8} = \frac{1}{4}$ (Diagram 3) $\frac{4}{8} = \frac{1}{2}$ (Diagram 4)
and $\frac{2}{4} = \frac{1}{2}$ (Diagram 4)

When fractions are different ways of describing the same part of a whole, we call them **equivalent fractions**.

Name the different ways of describing the parts of these shapes.

Give as many answers as possible.

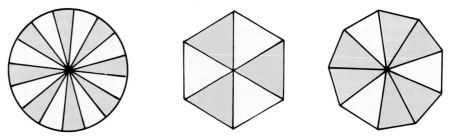

Did you find them all?

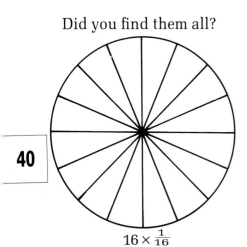

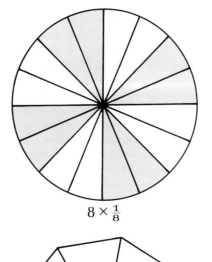

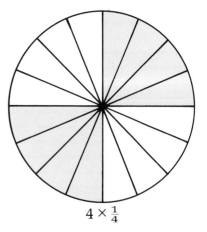

$$16 \times \tfrac{1}{16} \qquad 8 \times \tfrac{1}{8} \qquad 4 \times \tfrac{1}{4}$$

40

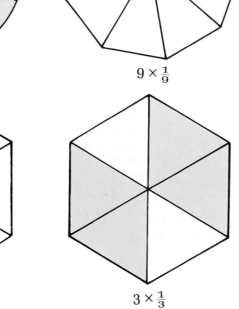

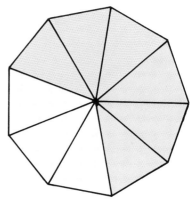

$$2 \times \tfrac{1}{2} \qquad 9 \times \tfrac{1}{9} \qquad 3 \times \tfrac{1}{3}$$

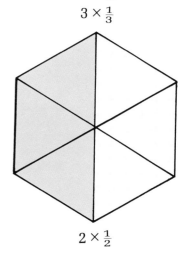

$$6 \times \tfrac{1}{6} \qquad\qquad 3 \times \tfrac{1}{3} \qquad\qquad 2 \times \tfrac{1}{2}$$

● You should be able to fill in these gaps now.

$$\tfrac{1}{2} = \tfrac{?}{6} \qquad \tfrac{1}{3} = \tfrac{2}{?} \qquad \tfrac{4}{6} = \tfrac{?}{3} \qquad \tfrac{2}{8} = \tfrac{?}{16} \qquad \tfrac{1}{?} = \tfrac{8}{16}$$

$$\tfrac{3}{?} = \tfrac{6}{8} \qquad \tfrac{9}{9} = ? \qquad \tfrac{3}{9} = \tfrac{?}{3}$$

Investigations

1. Draw a 5″ square on a piece of scrap paper. Divide it as shown. Label the pieces and cut them out. You should have eight wholes and eight quarters.

● Use them to display a set of five different mixed numbers. A mixed number is one which has a whole number part and a fraction part, like $5\frac{1}{3}$. You must use all the pieces. Each mixed number must be different from the others. Your set will add up to the ten wholes you started with. You must only use each piece once.

1 WHOLE			
1 WHOLE			
1 WHOLE			
1 WHOLE			
1 WHOLE			
1 WHOLE			
1 WHOLE			
1 WHOLE			
¼	¼	¼	¼
¼	¼	¼	¼

2. On scrap paper, draw a strip $6\frac{1}{4}$″ long and $\frac{1}{2}$″ wide. Mark it off in sections as shown in the diagram below.

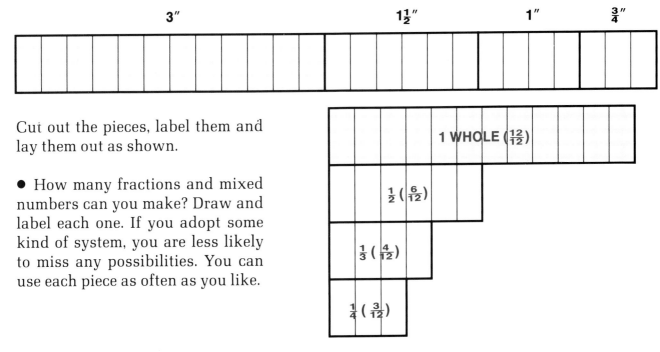

Cut out the pieces, label them and lay them out as shown.

● How many fractions and mixed numbers can you make? Draw and label each one. If you adopt some kind of system, you are less likely to miss any possibilities. You can use each piece as often as you like.

How much pie is left?

You eat $\frac{1}{3}$ of the pie for lunch

and another $\frac{1}{4}$ for supper

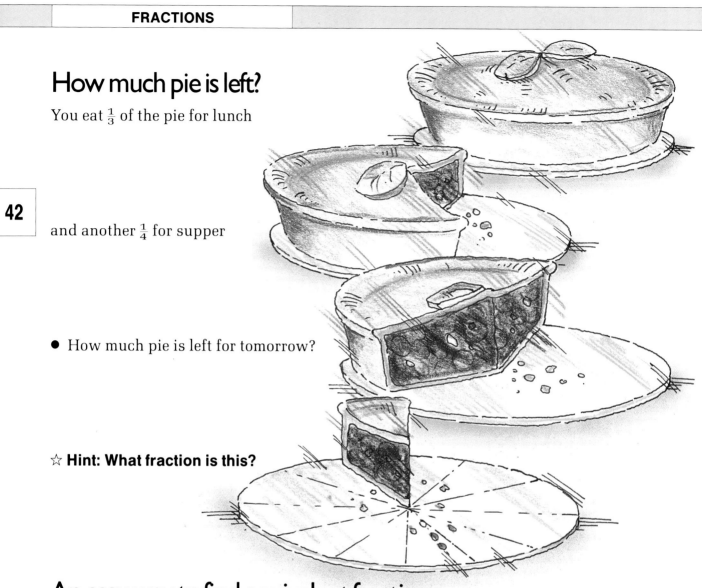

● How much pie is left for tomorrow?

☆ **Hint: What fraction is this?**

An easy way to find equivalent fractions

1. On graph paper, draw a horizontal and a vertical line from the bottom left hand corner. Label the horizontal line **Denominator** – the denominator of a fraction is the number beneath the dividing line. It tells us how many parts the whole has been divided into.

2. Label the vertical line **Numerator** – the numerator of a fraction is the number above the dividing line. It tells us how many of the parts there are.

3. Mark in the counting numbers from 0 along the bottom and up the side where the lines of the squares on the paper meet your lines.

4. Mark a dot at the point 10 across, 10 up. Carefully rule a line passing through 0 and the dot. This line represents all the ways of writing 1 as a fraction; for example, $\frac{10}{10}$ $\frac{2}{2}$ $\frac{7}{7}$ and so on.

5. To draw in the line for all the fractions equivalent to a half, mark a dot 10 across and 5 up ($\frac{5}{10}$). Draw the line which passes through 0 and the dot.

6. You can now read all the other values for $\frac{1}{2}$, wherever the $\frac{1}{2}$ line passes through the corner of a square; for example, $\frac{7}{14}$

7. Draw in the other lines using the points shown.

● **1.** Look at the line which passes through A. Write down the numerator and denominator at A. Repeat for another point on the line. What fraction does this line represent?

● **2.** What fraction do the lines through B and C represent?

Finding all the fractions in a group and arranging them in order of size

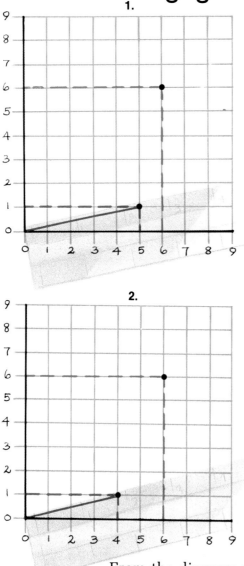

1.

2.

3.

You can also use the graph to build up a series of fractions in order of size.

1. To find all the fractions whose denominator is less than 6, lightly mark the point where 6 across meets 6 up.

2. Place a ruler along the denominator line. Rotate it counter-clockwise, taking care to keep one end on 0, until the ruler reaches the point you marked. Record each fraction, that is each time the ruler meets the corner of a square. If there are two squares on the same line, choose the one nearest to 0.

From the diagram you can see that we obtain the fractions

$$\frac{1}{5} \quad \frac{1}{4} \quad \frac{1}{3} \quad \frac{2}{5} \quad \frac{1}{2} \quad \frac{3}{5} \quad \frac{2}{3} \quad \frac{3}{4} \quad \text{and} \quad \frac{4}{5}$$

These are all the possible fractions with a denominator less than 6, and they are arranged in size from the smallest to the largest.

● List a similar series of fractions with denominator less than 7.

Help with adding and subtracting fractions

Use graph paper to make two different colored copies of this fraction chart. Cut one chart up and label each piece.

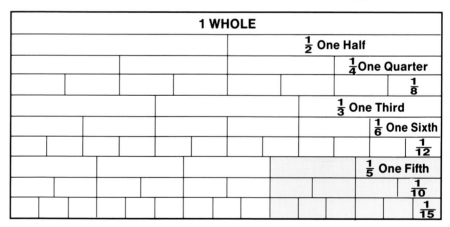

To do the sum $\frac{2}{5} + \frac{1}{3}$, take two $\frac{1}{5}$ pieces and one $\frac{1}{3}$ piece and see where you can fit them side by side on your chart. You will find that they exactly fit eleven of the $\frac{1}{15}$ spaces. This shows you that $\frac{2}{5} + \frac{1}{3} = \frac{11}{15}$

You can also see from your chart that $\frac{2}{5} = \frac{4}{10} = \frac{6}{15}$

● Try these sums using your fraction chart:

$\frac{1}{4} + \frac{1}{3}$

$\frac{2}{6} + \frac{3}{12}$

$\frac{1}{2} + \frac{2}{5}$

$\frac{1}{2} + \frac{1}{6}$ (write the answer to this one in two ways)

$\frac{3}{10} + \frac{2}{5}$

Answers on page 46

Check to see if you answered the questions on page 45 correctly.

When you have, try the sums below.

In some of them you will have a whole number as well as a fraction in your answer.

For example: $\frac{1}{2} + \frac{5}{8} = \frac{4}{8} + \frac{5}{8} = 1\frac{1}{8}$

Answers to page 45

$\frac{1}{4} + \frac{1}{3} = \frac{7}{12}$

$\frac{2}{6} + \frac{3}{12} = \frac{7}{12}$

$\frac{1}{2} + \frac{2}{5} = \frac{9}{10}$

$\frac{1}{2} + \frac{1}{6} = \frac{4}{6} = \frac{2}{3}$

$\frac{3}{10} + \frac{2}{5} = \frac{7}{10}$

1 WHOLE														

	$\frac{1}{2}$ One Half
	$\frac{1}{4}$ One Quarter
	$\frac{1}{8}$
	$\frac{1}{3}$ One Third
	$\frac{1}{6}$ One Sixth
	$\frac{1}{12}$
	$\frac{1}{5}$ One Fifth
	$\frac{1}{10}$
	$\frac{1}{15}$

● For you to do:

$\frac{2}{3} + \frac{4}{6}$ $\frac{3}{5} + \frac{5}{10}$ $\frac{3}{4} + \frac{4}{12}$

$\frac{8}{15} + \frac{2}{3}$ (write the answer to this one in two ways)

$\frac{8}{10} + \frac{1}{3}$

Investigation

● How can you use your chart to subtract (take away) fractions? Try and figure out these.

$\frac{1}{2} - \frac{1}{4}$ $\frac{1}{2} - \frac{1}{3}$ $\frac{1}{3} - \frac{1}{5}$

$\frac{1}{4} - \frac{1}{8}$ $\frac{3}{4} - \frac{5}{12}$ $\frac{2}{3} - \frac{8}{15}$

Puzzle

● Can you divide this shape into four quarter pieces?

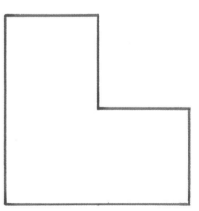

☆ **Hint – how can equivalent fractions help?**

Decimal fractions

Decimals are special fractions which are based on the idea of splitting a whole into ten parts, a hundred parts, a thousand parts and so on. You can think of it as looking at a number line with stronger and stronger magnifying glasses.

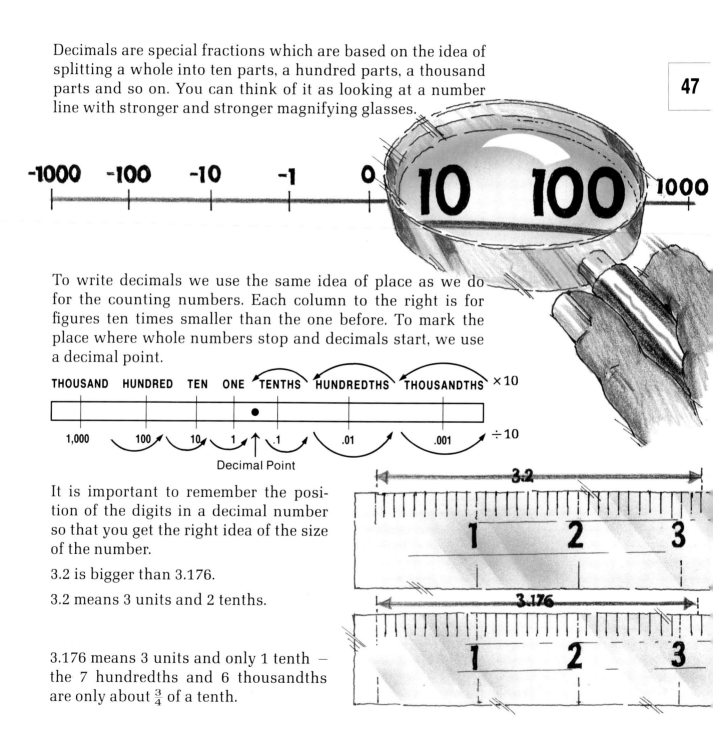

To write decimals we use the same idea of place as we do for the counting numbers. Each column to the right is for figures ten times smaller than the one before. To mark the place where whole numbers stop and decimals start, we use a decimal point.

THOUSAND	HUNDRED	TEN	ONE	TENTHS	HUNDREDTHS	THOUSANDTHS	×10
1,000	100	10	1	.1	.01	.001	÷10

Decimal Point

It is important to remember the position of the digits in a decimal number so that you get the right idea of the size of the number.

3.2 is bigger than 3.176.

3.2 means 3 units and 2 tenths.

3.176 means 3 units and only 1 tenth — the 7 hundredths and 6 thousandths are only about $\frac{3}{4}$ of a tenth.

To remind ourselves of this, we say 3.176 as "three point one seven six," NOT "three point one hundred and seventy six."

● How do you say 10.12 and 14.002?

Changing fractions to decimal fractions

48

Any fraction can be changed into a decimal fraction.
The fraction $\frac{1}{2}$ means 1 divided by 2. The fraction line means the same as the division sign – if you put a · above and below, it is the same.

$$\frac{1}{2} \text{ means } 1 \div 2$$

To convert to a decimal fraction, we solve the following problem.

$$2\overline{\smash{\big)}1.0}^{.}$$

We can write 1.0 instead of 1 because they mean the same thing – one unit and no more. We must keep the decimal point in line in the problem and in the answer, so put it in before you forget.

"Two's into one don't go, so put zero in the answer and carry one to the next column. Two's into ten go five."

$$2\overline{\smash{\big)}1.0}^{0.5}$$

You can check your answer with a calculator. Put 1 into the display, press $\div$ and then 2 and $=$

It is a good idea to put a zero before the decimal if there is no whole number part. It is not easy to notice a decimal point at the beginning of a number.

Write 0.5 not .5.

● Try changing these fractions into decimals, first without and then with a calculator:

$\frac{1}{5}$ $\frac{1}{10}$ $\frac{2}{10}$ $\frac{2}{5}$ and $\frac{3}{5}$

Sometimes we need more than one 0 after the decimal point. To change $\frac{1}{4}$ into a decimal set out the sum

$$4 \overline{)1.0}$$

this works out as

$$\overset{0.2 \text{ r } 2}{4 \overline{)1.0}}$$

but we don't use remainders with decimals. Instead we add another 0 and carry the 2.

Doing this, we get

$$\overset{0.25}{4 \overline{)1.00}}$$

● Add as many 0's as you need to change these fractions to decimals.

$\frac{3}{4}$ $\frac{1}{8}$ $\frac{5}{8}$ $\frac{1}{100}$ $\frac{3}{100}$

Check your answers with a calculator.

What happens when you try to change $\frac{1}{3}$ into a decimal?

$$\overset{0.3333....}{3 \overline{)1.0000}}$$

You find that however many zero's you use, you still keep getting a remainder of 1.

0.3333.... is a **recurring decimal** and we write a line above the 3 to show that it repeats endlessly.

$$\frac{1}{3} = 0.\overline{3}$$

To write

$$\tfrac{1}{3} = 0.\overline{3}$$

might not seem a very accurate answer.

But remember what the line over the 3 means – there are as many 3's as you wish to write. The second 3 after the decimal point means $\tfrac{3}{100}$. This is a tiny part of an inch, for example.

50

Most of the time, two figures after the decimal point give as much accuracy as we need. If we need more, we can go as far as we like.

● What would these fractions be as decimals?

$\tfrac{2}{3}$ $\tfrac{1}{6}$ (Put the line over the figure which repeats.)

$\tfrac{1}{9}$ (Now you can see why the line is important.)

$\tfrac{5}{6}$ $\tfrac{5}{9}$

$\tfrac{1}{7}$ (You need to keep going for this one! Put a line above all of the figures which repeat.)

Investigation

Find the decimal equivalents of $\tfrac{1}{2}$ $\tfrac{1}{3}$ $\tfrac{1}{4}$ $\tfrac{1}{5}$ $\tfrac{1}{6}$ and so on, up to at least $\tfrac{1}{21}$ Record your results and note whether or not they are recurring decimals.

You will need to figure out some of them with pencil and paper, because an 8-digit display calculator will not show enough of the pattern.

● Can you see a rule which will tell you whether or not a fraction will turn into a recurring decimal?

● Does your rule work for numerators other than 1?

Negative Numbers

The number line contains fractions of whole numbers as well as the counting numbers and zero. There is no reason why we should not count backward from zero as well as forward.

We call the numbers less than zero negative numbers. To distinguish them from positive, or ordinary numbers, we put a minus sign in front. This shows they are subtracted from zero.

We are quite used to this in everyday life. You could think of a thermometer as a number line on its side.

We talk about a temperature of "minus 10" or "10 below."

● What are the temperatures shown on these thermometers?

Another way we use the idea of negative numbers is when we owe money.

I write out a check for $120.

I only have $100 in the bank.

I am $20 overdrawn.

$100 - 120 = -20$

52

When bank ledgers were kept by hand, before the introduction of calculators and computers, the money taken out of the account was written in red ink. If you took out more than you had put in, you were "in the red."

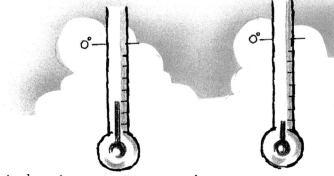

Adding negative numbers

● If the temperature was at -5 and it falls another 2 degrees, what is the new temperature?

This drop in temperature can be written as
$$-5 + -2 = -7$$

Later in the day, the sun comes out and the temperature rises 8 degrees. What is the temperature now?
$$-7 + 8 = 1$$

We can do the same problem with money.

I owe my sister $5 and then borrow another $2 from my Mom to buy Dad's birthday present. Now I owe $7.

I win $8 in a poster competition. Now I can pay back $7 and have $1 left.

● Try these;

1. $-4 + -5 = ?$ **2.** $-1 + -? = -8$ **3.** $1 + -3 = ?$

4. $10 + -16 = ?$ **5.** $32 + -? = -1$ **6.** $-? + -7 = -10$

Another way of understanding negative numbers is to fill in an addition table.

● Copy the table and continue the patterns in the rows and columns.

SECOND NUMBER

+	5	4	3	2	1	0	−1	−2	−3	−4	−5
5	10	9	8	7	6	5	4	3	2	1	0
4	9	8	7	6	5	4	3	2	1	0	−1
3	8	7	6	5	4	3	2	1	0	−1	−2
2	7	6	5	4	3	2	1	0	−1	−2	−3
1	6	5	4	3	2	1	0	−1	−2	−3	−4
0	5	4	3	2	1	0	−1	−2	−3	−4	−5
−1	4	3	2	1	0	−1					
−2	3	2	1	0	−1	−2					
−3	2	1	0	−1	−2	−3					
−4	1	0	−1	−2	−3	−4					
−5	0	−1	−2	−3	−4	−5					

FIRST NUMBER

Turn to page 56.

Playing with negative numbers

To play on the board on the opposite page, you need a die and a coin and a counter for each player.

Each player places his or her counter on the START square. In turn, each player throws the die and tosses the coin. The die tells you the number of squares to move your counter. The coin tells you the direction in which to move. Heads numbers move forward toward the positive numbers. Tails numbers move backward toward the negative numbers.

If you throw tails and 5 on your first turn, you move your counter backward five spaces from START to −5. If you throw heads and 3 on your next go, you move forward three spaces to land on −2.

The instruction on the −2 square tells you to ADD 4 so you move your counter four spaces toward the positive numbers to 2.

The first player to reach either HOME square is the winner. If a counter lands on a square already occupied by a counter, the counter on the square is moved back or forward to START.

Were you right?

Check your answers to the problems on page 53 using the table.

SECOND NUMBER

+	5	4	3	2	1	0	−1	−2	−3	−4	−5
5	10	9	8	7	6	5	4	3	2	1	0
4	9	8	7	6	5	4	3	2	1	0	−1
3	8	7	6	5	4	3	2	1	0	−1	−2
2	7	6	5	4	3	2	1	0	−1	−2	−3
1	6	5	4	3	2	1	0	−1	−2	−3	−4
0	5	4	3	2	1	0	−1	−2	−3	−4	−5
−1	4	3	2	1	0	−1	−2	−3	−4	−5	−6
−2	3	2	1	0	−1	−2	−3	−4	−5	−6	−7
−3	2	1	0	−1	−2	−3	−4	−5	−6	−7	−8
−4	1	0	−1	−2	−3	−4	−5	−6	−7	−8	−9
−5	0	−1	−2	−3	−4	−5	−6	−7	−8	−9	−10

FIRST NUMBER

**Turn back to page 55 to play
the board game.**

A playground game

Mark out a number line from +10 to −10 in chalk on the ground. The players line up behind each other, in line with 0.

A caller asks an addition problem which includes the number at which the players are standing. The last player to stand in the correct answer line each time is out, until only the winner remains.

A possible sequence is:

$0 + -3$

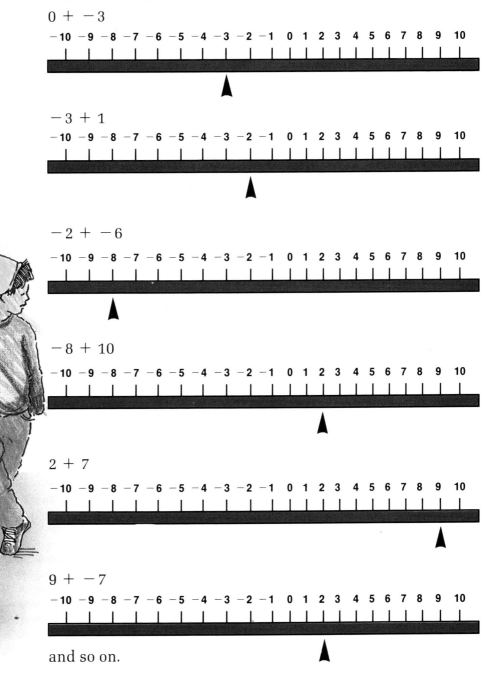

$-3 + 1$

$-2 + -6$

$-8 + 10$

$2 + 7$

$9 + -7$

and so on.

Subtracting negative numbers

Copy and complete the subtraction table. Use the patterns in the rows and columns to fill in any answers you don't know.

SECOND NUMBER

	5	4	3	2	1	0	-1	-2	-3	-4	-5
5				3	4	5					
4											
3			0								
2											
1					0	1					
0						0					
-1	-6										
-2											
-3											
-4											
-5	-10										

FIRST NUMBER

Use the table to help you with these examples.

$4 - -2 = ?$ $3 - -5 = ?$ $0 - -3 = ?$ $2 - -1 = ?$

$4 + 2 = ?$ $3 + 5 = ?$ $0 + 3 = ?$ $2 + 1 = ?$

● What do you notice?

You can now change the playground game to include subtractions.

Multiplying and dividing negative numbers

Copy and complete the multiplication table. Color the negative numbers in red.

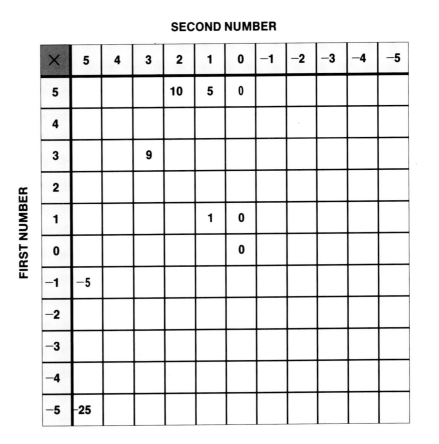

SECOND NUMBER

×	5	4	3	2	1	0	−1	−2	−3	−4	−5
5				10	5	0					
4											
3			9								
2											
1					1	0					
0						0					
−1	−5										
−2											
−3											
−4											
−5	−25										

FIRST NUMBER (left side label)

● What are the missing signs in this table?

×	+	−
+	+	?
−	?	?

● Is the result of multiplying together a positive and a negative number, a positive or a negative number?

● Is the result of multiplying together two negative numbers, a positive or a negative number?

You can work backwards through the multiplication table to find the answers to division problems.

● Are the rules about signs, when dividing negative numbers, the same as for multiplication?

Glossary

base the size of group used for counting. Base ten uses groups of ten. Ten units make one ten; ten tens make one hundred and so on.

binary arithmetic arithmetic which counts in groups of two's. Its most common use is in computers.

decimals special fractions which divide a whole number into tenths, hundredths, thousandths and so on.

denary arithmetic arithmetic which counts in groups of ten. This is the arithmetic we commonly use.

denominator the number underneath the line in a fraction.

digit a finger or toe; a numeral from 0 to 9.

equivalent fractions fractions with different numbers which mean the same size part of a whole.
For example, $\frac{15}{30} = \frac{5}{10} = \frac{4}{8} = \frac{1}{2}$ are equivalent fractions.

factor a number which divides another number into equal parts. 1, 2, 3 and 6 are factors of 6. 4 and 5 are not.

fraction a whole number can be divided into equal parts. These parts are fractions.

integer a whole number.

multiple the multiples of a number are the numbers which it will divide into exactly, with no remainder. The multiples of 3 are 3, 6, 9 12, 15, 18 and so on.

numerator the number above the line in a fraction.

prime number a number which cannot be divided exactly by any other number except 1.

recurring decimals numbers in which the decimal part ends in a number, or a group of numbers, which endlessly repeat.

subtraction taking away one number from another.

Answers

Page 9

The chart shows the symbols which early civilizations used for recording numbers.

Page 10

You might find Roman numerals on grave stones, old coins, sundials, or inscriptions as well as on watches and clocks. Television programs and movies sometimes have the date on which they were made in Roman numerals.

An advantage of the Arabic number system is that you only need to learn ten symbols. It is the only one to use zero to form new numbers. A disadvantage is that the numerals do not look like the number of things they stand for. This makes them harder to learn and remember.

1. 3   **2.** 11   **3.** 6   **4.** 24   **5.** 59   **6.** 40   **7.** 218   **8.** 21   **9.** 456   **10.** 85

Puzzle One possibility is

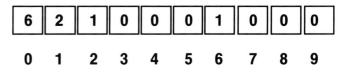

You may have found others which work.

Page 13

The next two numbers are

If you place a mirror vertically down the middle of each symbol, you will see the answer.

Page 18

When the ten o'clock train is three hours late and arrives at one o'clock.

Roman and Mayan symbols change at 5.

The Egyptian, Babylonian and Roman symbols change at 10.

The Mayans used 20 as a special number. Perhaps they counted their toes also.

There are 6 60's in 360.

Page 19

256 seeds = 1 priest

256	64	16	4	1
p	**g**	**t**	**f**	**s**

1. 28 **2.** 771 **3.** 532 **4.** 39

Page 22

$64 + 32 + 16 + 8 + 4 + 2 + 1 = 127$

Page 23

The third house is number 6.

House 15 would be opposite house 16.

Page 24

+	ODD	EVEN
ODD	EVEN	ODD
EVEN	ODD	EVEN

The two odd 1's in each odd number join together to form one group of 2.

Page 25

1. You can tell who will win, unless the potential loser forces a draw.

2. If no moves away from B are allowed, the second player will always win.

3. If it takes an odd number of moves to get from A to B, the first player will win.

4. Who will win depends on whether the number of moves from A to B is odd or even.

5. $1 + 3 + 5 + 11 = 20$

6. $1 + 2 + 3 + 4 = 10$

7. You need to add 1 to any odd number to make it even.

8. 2 is the smallest number to turn odd to even by multiplying.

9. ODD = ODD × ODD

10. No. $\frac{1}{2}$ of 4 is even; $\frac{1}{2}$ of 6 is odd.

11. $17 + 19 + 21 + 23 = 80$

12. Seven (take away one letter!)

13. Eleven (take away two letters!)

Page 27

There are 4 primes below 10,

8 below 20,

10 below 30

and 12 below 40.

Page 31

1309 is not prime. $1309 = 17 \times 77$

119 is not prime. $7 \times 17 = 119$

283 is prime.

221 is not prime $221 = 13 \times 17$

No $(20 \times 6) + 1 = 121 = 11 \times 11$

$(20 \times 6) - 1 = 119 = 7 \times 17$

3, 7, 13, 37

Page 33

1. No **2.** Yes **3.** No **4.** No **5.** Yes **6.** Yes
7. No **8.** No **9.** No **10.** Yes **11.** Yes **12.** No
13. No **14.** Yes **15.** Yes **16.** Yes **17.** Yes
18. Yes **19.** Yes **20.** Yes **21.** Yes **22.** No

Page 37

$99\frac{9}{9}$

Page 38

$A = \frac{1}{4}$ $\quad B = \frac{1}{8}$ $\quad C = \frac{1}{12}$ $\quad D = \frac{1}{24}$

Page 40

$\frac{1}{2} = \frac{3}{16}$ $\quad \frac{1}{3} = \frac{2}{6}$ $\quad \frac{4}{6} = \frac{2}{3}$ $\quad \frac{2}{8} = \frac{4}{16}$ $\quad \frac{1}{2} = \frac{8}{16}$

$\frac{3}{4} = \frac{6}{8}$ $\quad \frac{9}{9} = \frac{1}{1} = 1$ $\quad \frac{3}{9} = \frac{1}{3}$

Page 41

Investigation 1

$1\frac{1}{4}$, $\quad 1\frac{1}{2}$, $\quad 1\frac{3}{4}$, $\quad 2\frac{1}{4}$, $\quad 3\frac{1}{4}$

Investigation 2

A total of 14 fractions

$\frac{1}{2}$, $\frac{1}{3}$, $\frac{1}{4}$, $\frac{10}{12}$ $(\frac{5}{6})$, $\frac{9}{12}$ $(\frac{3}{4})$, $\frac{7}{12}$, $1\frac{1}{2}$, $1\frac{1}{3}$, $1\frac{1}{4}$, $1\frac{5}{6}$, $1\frac{3}{4}$,

one $\frac{7}{12}$, one $\frac{1}{12}$, two $\frac{1}{12}$'s.

Page 42

$\frac{5}{12}$ is left for tomorrow.

Page 43

1. The line through **A** represents $\frac{1}{5}$
2. The lines through **B** and **C** represent $\frac{1}{3}$ and $\frac{3}{4}$ respectively.

Page 44

Fractions with a denominator less than 7 are $\frac{1}{6}$ $\frac{1}{5}$ $\frac{1}{4}$ $\frac{1}{3}$ $\frac{2}{5}$ $\frac{1}{2}$ $\frac{3}{5}$ $\frac{2}{3}$ $\frac{3}{4}$ $\frac{4}{5}$ $\frac{5}{6}$

Page 46

$\frac{2}{3} + \frac{4}{6} = 1\frac{1}{3} = 1\frac{2}{6}$

$\frac{3}{5} + \frac{5}{10} = 1\frac{1}{10}$

$\frac{3}{4} + \frac{4}{12} = 1\frac{1}{12}$

$\frac{8}{15} + \frac{2}{3} = 1\frac{3}{15} = 1\frac{1}{5}$

$\frac{8}{10} + \frac{1}{3} = 1\frac{2}{15}$

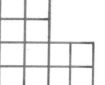

$\frac{1}{2} - \frac{1}{4} = \frac{1}{4}$

$\frac{1}{2} - \frac{1}{3} = \frac{1}{6}$

$\frac{1}{3} - \frac{1}{5} = \frac{2}{15}$

$\frac{1}{4} - \frac{1}{8} = \frac{1}{8}$

$\frac{3}{4} - \frac{5}{12} = \frac{4}{12} = \frac{1}{3}$

$\frac{2}{3} - \frac{8}{15} = \frac{2}{15}$

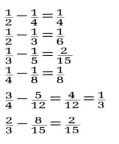

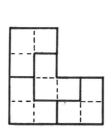

Page 49

$\frac{1}{5} = 0.2$ $\qquad \frac{3}{4} = 0.75$

$\frac{1}{10} = 0.1$ $\qquad \frac{1}{8} = 0.125$

$\frac{2}{10} = 0.2$ $\qquad \frac{5}{8} = 0.625$

$\frac{2}{5} = 0.4$ $\qquad \frac{1}{100} = 0.01$

$\frac{3}{5} = 0.6$ $\qquad \frac{3}{100} = 0.03$

Page 50

$\frac{2}{3} = 0.\overline{6}$ $\quad \frac{1}{6} = 0.1\overline{6}$ $\quad \frac{1}{9} = 0.\overline{1}$ $\quad \frac{5}{6} = 0.8\overline{3}$

$\frac{5}{9} = 0.\overline{5}$ $\quad \frac{1}{7} = 0.\overline{142857}$

Your rule should be something like this: the denominator must have no prime factors other than 2 and 5, or else it will repeat.

The rule only works for numerators other than 1 if you reduce the fraction to its simplest form. For example, $\frac{3}{6} = \frac{1}{2}$

Page 51

-2, -7 and -10

Page 53

1. $-4 + -5 = -9$
2. $-1 + -7 = -8$
3. $1 + -3 = -2$
4. $10 + -16 = -6$
5. $32 + -33 = -1$
6. $-3 + -7 + -10$

Page 58

Subtracting a negative number gives the same result as adding a positive number.

Page 59

The product of a positive and a negative number is a negative number.

The product of two negative numbers is a positive number.

Yes, the rules are the same.

×	+	−
+	+	−
−	−	+

Index

64